Bizarre Behaviour

IN ANCIENT GREECE

©2024
BookLife Publishing Ltd.
King's Lynn, Norfolk
PE30 4LS, UK

All rights reserved.
Printed in India.

A catalogue record for this book is available from the British Library.

ISBN: 978-1-80505-605-8

Written by:
Shalini Vallepur
Adapted by:
Noah Leatherland
Edited by:
Elise Carraway
Designed by:
Jasmine Pointer

All facts, statistics, web addresses and URLs in this book were verified as valid and accurate at time of writing. No responsibility for any changes to external websites or references can be accepted by either the author or publisher.

AN INTRODUCTION TO BOOKLIFE RAPID READERS...

Packed full of gripping topics and twisted tales, BookLife Rapid Readers are perfect for older children looking to propel their reading up to top speed. With three levels based on our planet's fastest animals, children will be able to find the perfect point from which to accelerate their reading journey. From the spooky to the silly, these roaring reads will turn every child at every reading level into a prolific page-turner!

CHEETAH
The fastest animals on land, cheetahs will be taking their first strides as they race to top speed.

MARLIN
The fastest animals under water, marlins will be blasting through their journey.

FALCON
The fastest animals in the air, falcons will be flying at top speed as they tear through the skies.

Photo Credits
Images are courtesy of Shutterstock.com. With thanks to Getty Images, Thinkstock Photo and iStockphoto.
COVER & RECURRING – Andrei Stepanov, JORDEN MARBLE, Nsit, Macrovector. 4–5 – SCStock, vkilikov. 6–7 – dinosmichail, Mazerath. 8–9 – Lucian Milasan, Zwiebackesser. 10–11 – Jean-Léon Gérôme, Public domain, via Wikimedia Commons, Authentic travel, lemono. 12–13 – Tim UR, aaltair, NotionPic. 14–15 – Steve Swayne, CC BY-SA 2.0 <https://creativecommons.org/licenses/by-sa/2.0/>, via Wikimedia Commons, INTREEGUE Photography, Valentyn Volkov. 16–17 – ONYXprj, Uwe Bergwitz, Gilmanshin, baldezh. 18–19 – Cavan-Images, Dima Moroz. 20–21 – garanga, Fabio Alcini. 22–23 – Getty Villa, CC BY-SA 2.0 <https://creativecommons.org/licenses/by-sa/2.0/>, via Wikimedia Commons, l i g h t p o e t, National Archaeological Museum of Athens, Public domain, via Wikimedia Commons, johavel. 24–25 – yiannisscheidt, Vadym Sh. 26–27 – Ververidis Vasilis, AngelaLouwe. 28–29 – Zwiebackesser, Nejdet Duzen, inspiring.team, Steinar. 30 – mapman.

CONTENTS

PAGE 4 Ancient Greece
PAGE 6 Gods and Goddesses
PAGE 8 Cruel Myths
PAGE 10 Thoughtful Philosophers
PAGE 12 Health and Sickness
PAGE 14 The Olympic Games
PAGE 16 Pretty Greeks
PAGE 18 Break a Leg
PAGE 20 Painters and Decorators
PAGE 22 Playing Games
PAGE 24 Shocks at Sparta
PAGE 28 Down in the Underworld
PAGE 30 Your Place in History
PAGE 31 Glossary
PAGE 32 Index

Words that look like this are explained in the glossary on page 31.

ANCIENT GREECE

Different groups of people have come and gone throughout history. A lot of them did some very bizarre things in their time.

The ancient Greeks lived from around 800 BCE to 146 BCE. Ancient Greece was made up of areas of land called poleis.

BCE means Before the Common Era. This is the time before the year 0.

Although ancient Greece was split into poleis, the people shared a culture. They spoke the same language, and many believed in the same gods and goddesses. Sometimes, the poleis went to war with one another.

Athens was an important polis. In 507 BCE, the leader of Athens set up a system called democracy. Democracy let citizens vote for their leaders.

GODS AND GODDESSES

The ancient Greeks believed in lots of gods and goddesses. Each one was linked to a different part of life. The ancient Greeks believed the gods could protect them or punish them.

Mount Olympus

The most important gods were thought to live at the top of Mount Olympus. They could look down on the humans from up there.

The ancient Greeks took **worship** very seriously. They made sure to worship the gods every day. The ancient Greeks often said prayers. They also had festivals to celebrate the gods.

Temple of Concordia

The ancient Greeks built lots of temples to worship the gods. They believed that the priests in these temples could get messages from the gods.

CRUEL MYTHS

The ancient Greeks had many myths about the gods punishing people. Many of these punishments could last forever.

Prometheus

A Greek man called Prometheus was said to have stolen fire from the gods. Zeus, the king of the gods, chained Prometheus to a rock as punishment. Every day, an eagle arrived, pecked Prometheus open and ate part of his insides.

Sisyphus was a cruel Greek king, so Zeus decided to punish him. Sisyphus was forced to push a boulder up a mountain. Every time he got near the top, the boulder rolled all the way back down.

Sisyphus

King Tantalus was invited to dinners with the gods. After they caught him stealing food, they punished him by making him hungry forever.

THOUGHTFUL PHILOSOPHERS

There were many philosophers in ancient Greece. Philosophers were people who thought about the world and how things worked. They could have some strange beliefs about life.

Diogenes

Diogenes believed that people should live a simple life close to nature. Diogenes walked around without any shoes, lived in a barrel and went to the toilet in the street.

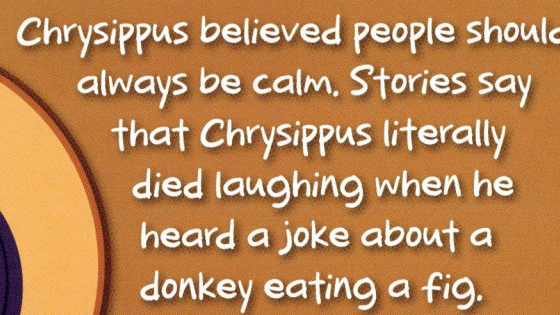

Chrysippus believed people should always be calm. Stories say that Chrysippus literally died laughing when he heard a joke about a donkey eating a fig.

Hippocrates believed certain liquids in the body controlled how someone felt. These were called the four humours. They were blood, phlegm, black bile and yellow bile. If someone's humours were not balanced, they would feel unwell.

HEALTH AND SICKNESS

Hippocrates' four humours helped doctors treat people. If someone had a headache, doctors believed they had too much blood. They cut them and let blood pour out!

Garlic was thought to **cure** a few eye problems in ancient Greece. Some doctors told people to put garlic on their eyelids. However, some doctors thought garlic would just make people fart.

Doctors used their sense of taste to learn more about someone's four humours. Doctors licked a sick person's vomit to find out what was happening inside their body.

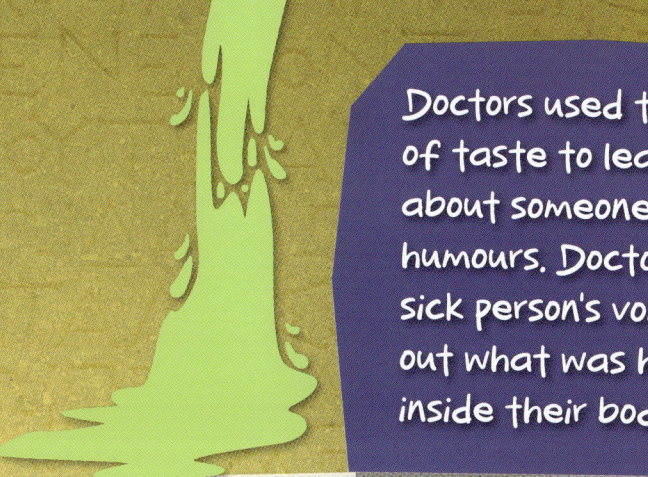

DO NOT TRY THIS YOURSELF!

Doctors did not just taste vomit. They would also taste the wee of a sick person. Apparently, healthy wee tasted just like fig juice.

THE OLYMPIC GAMES

The ancient Greeks invented the Olympic Games. They were held in Olympia. Athletes competed in the games to honour the gods and goddesses of Mount Olympus.

Olympia

Ancient Olympic athletes competed in events such as running, jumping, chariot racing, horse racing, discus throwing, wrestling and boxing. Most of the athletes who competed had to do it completely naked!

Ancient Greeks believed that the sweat of the Olympic athletes had special powers. The athletes were covered in olive oil before they exercised. Afterwards, the olive oil, sweat and dirt on their bodies was scraped off. This mixture was called gloios. It was poured into bottles and sold as a medicine.

PRETTY GREEKS

The ancient Greeks liked to look nice.

Crocodile poo was used to make a cream for keeping people free of wrinkles. The ancient Greeks sat in bathtubs full of mud and crocodile poo to help their skin.

Some women used a black powder called soot to give themselves unibrows. One long eyebrow was a sign of being clever.

The ancient Greeks found a way to turn their hair blonde. Some of them covered their hair in vinegar and left it to dry in the sunshine.

Greek gods and heroes were usually shown with big, curly beards. Men wanted to look just as cool as the gods. Some men heated metal tongs and used them to curl their beards.

BREAK A LEG

Ancient Greeks enjoyed going to the theatre. Every year, they had a festival in Athens to celebrate the god Dionysus. Thousands of people gathered in a theatre called the Odeon to watch plays.

Only men were allowed to act in plays. The actors wore masks and tall shoes. This meant that people farther back in the audience could see them.

There were two types of plays in ancient Greece.

Tragedies were serious plays where bad things happened. In *Oedipus the King*, the character Oedipus ends up killing his father and accidentally marrying his mother!

Comedies were funny plays where silly things happened. In comedies, the actors wore ridiculous outfits to make them look even sillier.

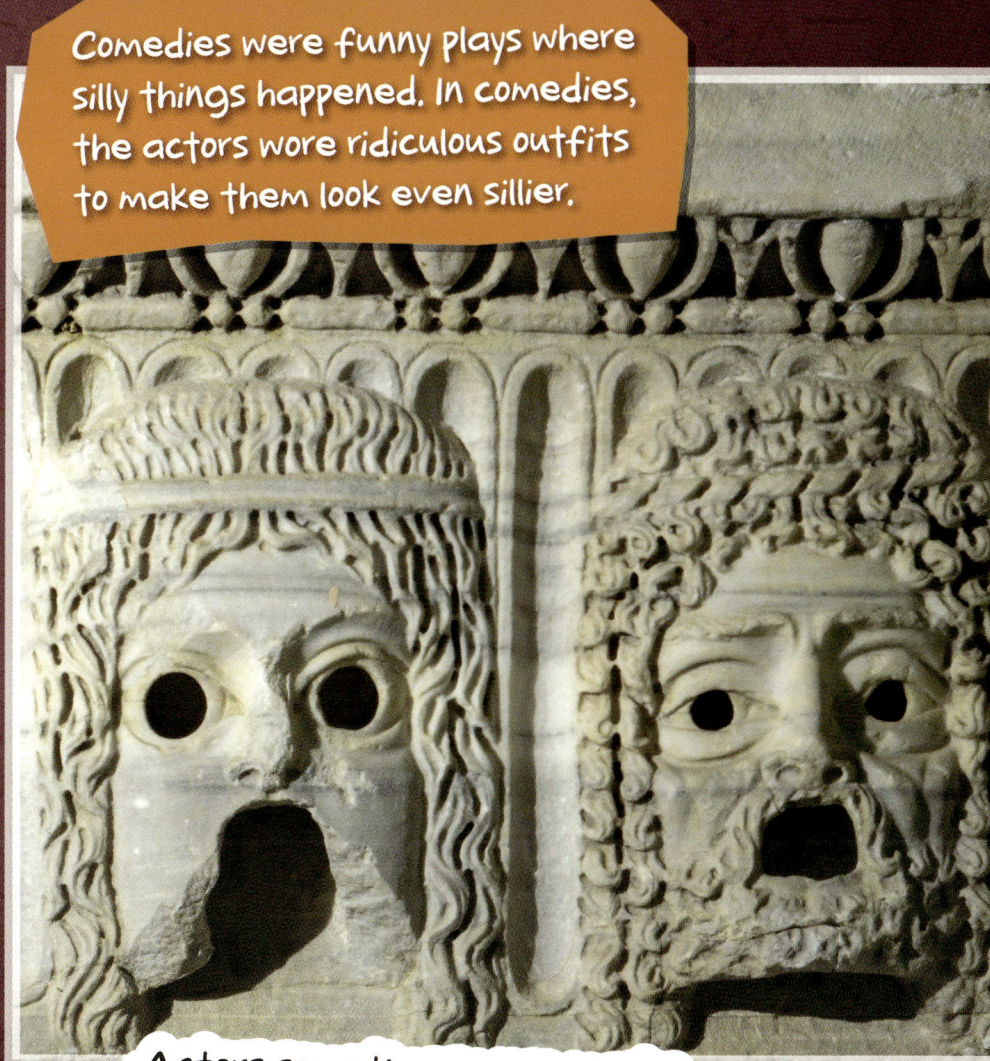

Actors sometimes wore masks.

PAINTERS AND DECORATORS

Ancient Greeks loved to make beautiful things and decorate the places they lived in.

Phidias was a famous sculptor. Phidias made a giant statue of Zeus for the god's temple in Olympia. He made the statue 12 metres tall and had it sitting on a throne made of gold and ivory. People travelled from all over Greece to see it.

The ancient Greeks loved to make pots. They painted their pots with scenes from the stories about their gods.

Pots had several uses. Rich people had a few different things to wipe their bums with. However, not everyone could afford them. Pots were cheap. Some ancient Greeks found that shards of smashed pots worked well to scrape a bum clean.

PLAYING GAMES

The ancient Greeks made lots of toys to play with. A lot of toys were made of a type of clay called terracotta.

Ancient Greeks played with yo-yos. They painted pictures of gods and goddesses on the sides of their yo-yos. Children decorated their dolls, too. They put human hair on their dolls' heads to make them look real.

The ancient Greeks played a ball game called episkyros. Players had to get the ball over the other team's line to win. The ball they played with was a blown-up pig's bladder.

Children gave their toys away when they got too old to play with them. Some kids took their old toys to temples and gave them to the gods.

SHOCKS AT SPARTA

Sparta was one of the poleis in ancient Greece. Spartan warriors were famous for being tough and brutal. Spartans did some strange things to keep their people strong.

Spartans made sure that their children were tough from a young age. Sometimes, newborn babies were left outside to see if they were strong enough to survive.

In many places in ancient Greece, girls were not allowed to do some of the things that boys did. However, the Spartans thought that all children had to be strong.

Girls were taught how to wrestle and played lots of sports. The Spartans believed that strong girls would grow up to have strong children of their own one day.

Boys went to a special school called an agoge. They were trained to become good soldiers. However, life was very tough in an agoge.

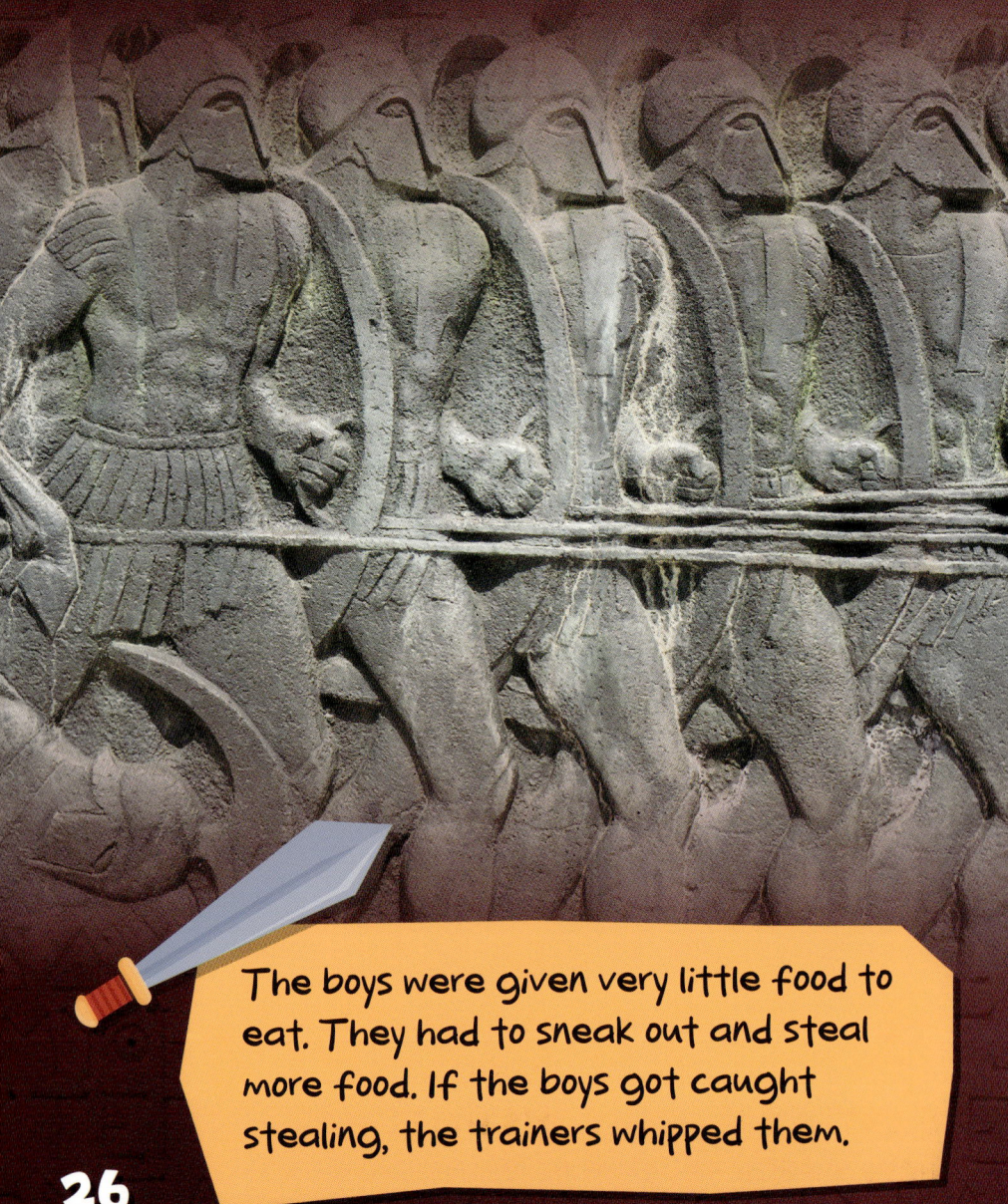

The boys were given very little food to eat. They had to sneak out and steal more food. If the boys got caught stealing, the trainers whipped them.

Boys were told tales to inspire them.

One story was about a Spartan boy who was looking for food and found a fox. The boy saw a trainer coming and did not want to get caught. He hid the fox under his shirt. The fox scratched his belly, but the boy stayed strong and acted like it did not hurt.

DOWN IN THE UNDERWORLD

The ancient Greeks believed in an afterlife. The first step was crossing the River Styx. The dead crossed the River Styx by paying a ferryman called Charon.

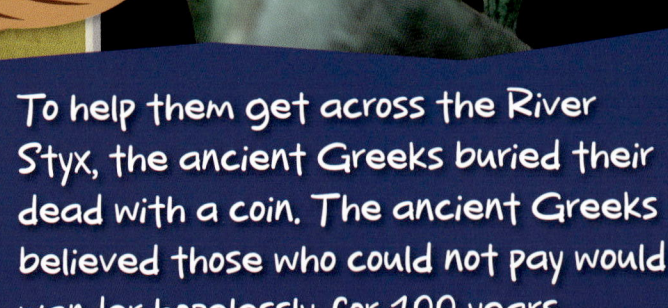

To help them get across the River Styx, the ancient Greeks buried their dead with a coin. The ancient Greeks believed those who could not pay would wander hopelessly for 100 years.

Once they were across the river, the dead had reached the underworld. Hades was the god of the underworld.

Ancient Greeks were often buried in places called necropolises.

Hades sent most people to the peaceful Asphodel Meadows. Brave heroes were sent to the Elysian Fields. People that the gods wanted to punish were sent to Tartarus.

YOUR PLACE IN HISTORY

Could you have lived in ancient Greece? Would you compete in the naked Olympics? Could you make it as a Spartan? Could you wipe your bum with broken pots?

If ancient Greece was too weird, you could live in another time period. But be warned! The strange things people did in other times might leave you thinking...

What bizarre behaviour!

GLOSSARY

AFTERLIFE — a place some people believe people go after they die

BILE — a yellowy or dark-green fluid in the stomach which helps break down food

BLADDER — the organ that holds and releases wee

CITIZENS — legally recognised members of a country

CURE — to heal someone and make them healthy again

INSPIRE — to influence or encourage someone to do something

LIQUIDS — materials that flow, such as water

MYTHS — traditional stories that may or may not be true

PHLEGM — a thick mucus, like snot

WORSHIP — a religious act where a person expresses praise for a god or gods

INDEX

Athens 5, 18
athletes 14–15
doctors 12–13
figs 11, 13
hair 17, 22
Mount Olympus 6, 14
plays 18–19
pots 21, 30
Spartans 24–25, 27, 30
temples 7, 20, 23
vomit 13
wee 13
Zeus 8–9, 20